Emerging

from dark confines.....into "life on wings"

by **Jane W. Lauber**

Copyright © 2014 by Jane W. Lauber

Emerging
from dark confines.....into "life on wings"
by Jane W. Lauber

Printed in the United States of America

ISBN 9781629521312

All rights reserved solely by the author. The author guarantees all contents are original and do not infringe upon the legal rights of any other person or work. No part of this book may be reproduced in any form without the permission of the author. The views expressed in this book are not necessarily those of the publisher.

Unless otherwise indicated, Bible quotations are taken from The Amplified Bible (AMP). Copyright © 1954, 1958, 1962, 1964, 1965, 1987 by The Lockman Foundation. Used by permission. All rights reserved.

www.xulonpress.com

Dedication

To my indescribably precious grandchildren,

Randy,

Michael,

Lisa,

Jessica, and

Jacob

(birth order)

And to their wonderful spouses—
And to my great grandchildren, yet to be born—

May the truths expressed in these writings and paintings help nourish the soil in which you are growing, until you complete God's perfect design for your lives.

And may my individual and inexpressible love for each of you be an affirming assurance all of your days.

Always and forever,

Your Nana xxxxxxooooooooo

Contents

To the Caterpillar	ix
Dedication	v
"Emerging" Introduction	xi
The Dust Bowl	13
The Pool	14
The Boxwoods	16
The Melody	17
The Rainbow	18
The Home	20
The Bluebird	23
The Cabin	24
The Long Road	26
The River	28
The Missed Trail	29
The Tree	31
The Sun	33
The Cat	35
The Flower	37
The Girl and the Dog	38
The House	40
The Turquoise Sea	42
The Answers	44
To the Curious Reader	47

To the Caterpillar

Little Worm, may I inquire…
What suggestions would inspire
Your choice of home where you reside
Without a window on a side?

To choose such darkness seems quite odd—
A sad mistake? Or act of God?
Deliberately to cramp one's style,
Encased, enclosed, so long a while!

Little Worm, you may confide
In me, who also must reside
In dark, constricted circumstance!
Not of my choice! But is it chance?

I squirm within such tight confines—
And beg an answer—Heaven declines
Its explanation. But I see
You, patiently content "to be!"

Then suddenly, it all is changed!
Your worm-like form is rearranged!
You have emerged! And now you fly
To "life on wings!"

LORD, so may I.

Emerging

"EMERGING"—the very word excites me. It conjures images of breaking out, or breaking through restricted confines and constricted movement. Of going from a cramped space into freedom—like a butterfly emerging from its dark cocoon and its tight, worm-like existence into life with wings.

It all is a process, and it all has purpose, although not without pain.

My journey has led and is leading through such a circumstance, and it is a continuing one. But now, I detect the sweet scent of the word, "emergence." And I <u>know</u>, that even "if I walk through the valley of the shadow of death," my skirt will twirl. That is because of the unfailing love and promises of God the Father; the blessed assurance of the salvation and presence of Jesus Christ, and the comfort, direction and power of the Holy Spirit. But that does not mean there is no struggle with thoughts and emotions, which must be taught courage and confidence. That is all part of our "continuing education."

The thoughts for these short vignettes came to me as I prayed. They are personal, and helped comfort and encourage me. It all began when my friend, Beverly, and I were on the telephone, praying. As she prayed for me, she saw a mental picture, a "vision," of a weary, sad little girl with her hands behind her back, kicking a tin can down a dusty road, with no green in sight. Beverly said that the area looked like a dust bowl. And that I was the little girl.

It was an <u>exact</u> description of how I was feeling, and it comforted me to know that the Lord understood. The next morning the words of the first line of the poem, "Dust Bowl" came to mind; a poem was en route— and the process has continued, with the ensuing images and ideas contained in these short pieces.

If you are in a dusty place on your journey, or if you are in transition into something new, or still in your "cocoon," I pray that these thoughts might encourage you as well. Although "emerging" is difficult, "life on wings" will be worth it.

The Dust Bowl

Kicking a can down a dusty road—
Traveling—but to where?
Aimless, purposeless, yet moving
To a shrouded "there."

My heart—somewhere in the can,
Gets kicked along as well.
 Bereft and battered, so confused,
I really cannot tell
If <u>dead</u> its dreams, or comatose?
If any beat at all
Responds to kicking of the tin,
Or hears the faintest call

Of <u>hope</u>, or <u>note</u> from distant sphere—
Or melody to say
"Keep moving, weary, broken child,
HE, too, has passed this way!"

*"O God, You are my God; earnestly will I seek You, My soul
thirsts for You, my flesh longs for You as in a dry and weary land, where no water is."*
(Psalm 63:1)

The Pool

A tiny woodland stream is flowing into a small pool. There are white stones beneath the waters as well as on the sides of the pool. Between the stones, purple, lily-like flowers are blooming. The sunlight catches and sparkles the moving water, which sounds like a soothing trickle. The ground around the pool is covered in soft green moss, accented with graceful fern. It is a little "oasis" indeed.

A very young, brown haired girl discovers the pool. She looks like the pretty little girl in the portrait, "Megan," which your friend and teacher, the master painter, Peter Granucci, painted years ago. In the portrait she stands barefoot, waist high in Black-eyed Susans.

But she is not so pretty now. She is dusty and very tired. She lies down beside the little pool, propped up on one elbow and begins sticking her fingers into the water to feel and taste it. She feels very, very alone.

She spots a gold fish swimming in the pool and tries to play with it with her fingers. Its bright gold catches the sunlight and glistens.

She sees a wide green leaf on the ground, and from it makes a cup from which she might sip the water. It tastes cool and sweet.

She lies on her back and looks up at the canopy of trees overhead and the rays of light streaming through them. She muses: "The stream, the little pool, the fresh water, and the gold fish...where did all these come from?"

A mighty voice emanating from the light, responds in a deep but gentle tone, *"From Me!"*

And she knows that she is <u>not</u> alone. And never would be again.

She lies down on the soft moss, closes her eyes and muses, "I wonder where that little stream is going? I hope it knows its destination, better than I know mine!"

As she dozes off to dream, she sees the little stream. It is flowing quietly, then cascading over large rocks, then joining another stream and then another, until she sees it merge with a river, who greets it with its welcoming waters.

She watches the river twisting and turning on its way, and in the far, far distance, she can see its destination—a beckoning, shimmering, sparkling turquoise sea. The stream will find its way, and she knows she will find hers as well.

The little girl is sleeping soundly now, resting on the soft moss and at peace.

As she dreams, and unknown to her because her eyes are tightly closed, a yellow butterfly encircles the sleeping child, and then flies away.

"See yourself, My child, as that little girl—"portrait perfect" in My beauty but weary and worn from the journey. Find the quiet, trickling pool and there, rest."

"Although you are in a dark place in your life, you are pushing through the difficulties, pain, and uncertainties as best you can, fully appreciating your many blessings. Know this: <u>Nothing</u> is wasted! I will use this time to give you insights which will promote deep healing within you. Some of the thoughts will relate to you as an adult; others, to the little girl within you in need of wholeness. Allow Me to change you as your journey, integrating and healing you."

"The contents of a broken vessel drain out through the cracks. So I would mend your brokenness that you may hold the sacred waters of My Presence, and be ready to pour out those waters for others, whose roads are dry and dusty also."

Your loving Father

My child, I want to give you hope for your future, for pleasures yet ahead. I want you to see one of My gardens!

The Boxwoods

The boxwoods are fragrant. The orderly rows of green, leafy globes line the garden walks, their leaves fresh and sparkling as the sunlight touches the morning dew.

You are surveying the garden to see what has just bloomed. You glance at the corner of the garden where something catches your eye. Quietly, you go and kneel beside a new-born fawn and her mother, cuddled together beneath the large oak tree in the corner of the garden.

Both the fawn and her mother are still and quiet, but respond to your voice and touch with open eyes, a little shudder and the twitch of a tail. You are awed at the beauty of the scene—the new birth, the freshly blooming flowers and the fragrance of the boxwoods.

The fountain in the central circle of the garden is large, with stately tiers. You step toward it on the brick walkways and sit on the edge of its large pool where you can feel the cool spray and watch as thousands of diamond droplets explode upward, then gently curve downward toward the pool—and splash into its dancing waters.
It is pristine, magical. It is like a dream come true.

So you, someday, shall explore the gardens of God which are yet in store for you, for I have promised:

> "Eye has not seen, nor has ear heard, neither has entered into the heart of man, what God has prepared for those who love Him."
>
> (I Corinthians 2:9)

The Melody

There is a melody, a song that you have heard somewhere—wisps of it gently brush your mind as you try to remember the tune, or where you have heard it. It is evasive, mysterious, yet it draws you as forcefully as gravity, with the misty memory of its sweet refrain. You strain to listen more intently to see if you can recall or even catch a faint sequence of its fleeting notes. But you cannot.

Eventually, you stop trying. The world's sounds and sights, the cacophony of indigestible noises which a planet makes in overdrive, muffle and even obscure a softly sung, whispered song of the past.

One day, walking with Me in the woods behind your log house, when your spirit is quiet, and your heart is tuned toward Me, you hear a sound. A soft breeze ripples the leaves and branches overhead. The sound is delicate, smooth like fine silk, soft like a billowy, almost nebulous pink cloud blown by the wind through the leaves. And then, you hear notes—only a few of them but enough to awaken the yearning of a heart starved for song.

They are notes from My song to you, My child. The angels sang, not only at the birth of My Son, but also at the birth of each of My sons and daughters. Each melody is unique; no two alike.

My song over you is still being sung. I know because I, Myself, sing it. It has as its refrain,

> *"I have loved you with an everlasting love, therefore with loving kindness I have drawn you." (Jeremiah 31:3)*

Hear the song, My child. Let its truth reverberate within your being. Let its sounds bring the soothing balm of heaven over your tired and ruptured heart. Let it express eternity—NOW—within you, to heal your diseases and restore your injured soul.

With love from your Singing God, your Father.

> *"He will rejoice over you with singing..."*
> (Zephaniah 3:17)

The Rainbow

There is a rainbow. The sky is full of its overarching beauty, its colors so deep and rich they look as if coming directly from heaven's glory.

They dazzle your sight, and then fade, but the memory, and even the photographs of the sight, continue to mesmerize with the wonder of those fleeting moments.

You have rejoiced and photographed many such rainbows, My child, in the natural world. And you have rejoiced and photographed many "rainbow moments" of exquisite pleasure with people, places, and sights which you have loved. These moments have faded as rainbows do, yet remain in memory to be cherished always.

However, there is pain that is attached to and accompanies, many of your cherished "rainbow memories," pain from loss and heart desolation associated with them. As if your heart has been emptied of its treasures by a thieving and malicious hand.

Yes, human choices and actions have been culprits, yet behind and allowing it all, there has been a Greater Hand, one which has held you precious from eternity past and has put a heart in you which rends—as does Mine—with rejection and distances between those you love and yourself.

And your unfulfilled dreams—painful, yes. But what birthed those dreams? Was it not hope of approval, rather than rejection from those whose approval mattered? Or even an inferior substitute for the pleasure of nearness to those whose nearness you crave. Or a tangible gift to Me of a worthy accomplishment, which might merit My favor?

All of these hopes and dreams dissolve in the ocean of My love for you, heartbreakingly expressed and generously given to you in Jesus.

So surrender to Me your all; not only your life and desires, but your pain, particularly that attached to the beautiful "rainbow memories" of human love, people, places and animals taken from you. As you do, the "rainbow memory" will remain to give you pleasure, yet from it will be extracted that pain which grieves your heart.

So as you give to Me, specifically, each pain associated with your memories, I will turn each downward arching "rainbow memory" into an upward curving smile—toward Me—your "Great Fulfiller."

                              Your Father

"Surely, He has borne our griefs and
carried our sorrows."
(Isaiah 53:4)

The Home

In your mind, several images of "home" enter and compete with one another for center stage of your imagination. Each is beautiful and appealing. Appearing first is the home in New Hampshire where your heart still lives in the memories of the "best years of our lives." It exits.

Next on stage comes a home, only roughly outlined, which you hope to have here in Florida. Although it is still waiting for its proper season, you imagine its floor plan and mentally decorate its spaces. It exits as well.

In clouded and far less distinct form, your ultimate home in heaven enters the stage. It is far too hazy to see details, but your imagination plays with how it might look and what it may contain.

None of these players on the stage really comfort you. The New Hampshire farm fills you with longing and sadness at its loss. The image of a hoped-for home here in Florida, brings questions about finances and impatience to find it. And the heavenly home seems a bit unreal, although you know it is not. But living there means dying here, and you are not quite ready for that. The curtains close.

You contemplate your situation as it is now. You are renting someone else's space which makes you feel dislocated. This is <u>their</u> home; not yours. This is <u>their</u> furniture, not your family antiques which remind you of your roots. Although it is lovely, this home seems more like a branch on which you have landed, temporarily, in your flight. You long to build a nest, not just for yourself, but for others to be blessed as well. But that desire is denied in this transition time.

Having recently moved to Florida, you are divested of your home, your health (having been diagnosed with stage 4 cancer), your husband (sick with Parkinson's for thirteen years, but now in Assisted Living because you are unable to continue to care for him); your art (as your business and passion); your church and prayer groups, your many friends and cordial neighbors and activities which made you feel like "you." Plus, financial loses have added uncertainties.

But you refuse self-pity or complaint! You are simply stating the facts of your present reality. You know very well that others are living in tragic circumstances by far more difficult and overwhelmingly heart-breaking than yours, and you are extremely thankful for your abounding blessings. With this move to Florida, you have gained nearness to your beloved family and that is immeasurable gain.

Still, you wonder what a "nest-builder" does when he cannot build a nest? You feel like a fish "beached" on the sand who flips around now and then hoping for a high wave to wash him back to familiar waters. And I hear the questions of your heart which ask, "If you can't go backward, and you can't go forward, and it's not time to go up—and you refuse to go "down," then what do you do?

And I would answer you and remind you that I and My Father promised to make our home within you—to "nest" in you. That <u>you</u> are a home for God on this earth! You decorate it as you choose, with those things that fill your heart and life, with both the lovely and the shabby. Hopefully, you keep your inner house clean for us, and in good repair, both the interior as well as the exterior. And you refuse to allow anything to enter this home which would violate our Holiness.

Yes, yours is an antique home, but we like antiques! Remember, We are "The Ancient of Days!" Your inner home is on heaven's "Historical Registry!"

Therefore, if the circumstances of this transition time prevent a "nest builder" from building a nest, why not focus on building and decorating your <u>inner home</u> for God? Why not give your attention to choosing the colors of your thoughts and actions to those that match God's tastes and desires—His longings for your love and attention? Why not turn your eyes away from your "lacks" and gaze on Him, and His beauty? And how you can love Him more and make Him more comfortable in your inner being? And purpose to fulfill His description of His house, that it would be called "a house of prayer." Praise and prayer make lovely décor!

So even though you cannot unpack your grandmother's china and serve guests, at this time, you can serve Me and My people by praying the prayers on My heart for those for whom I died.

Therefore make that "inner home" in your heart of hearts the "nest" you build. Not just for yourself, and for the family of God, but for Me—for God Himself—for the Godhead to feel loved and "at home!"

The curtains reopen on the stage of your mind. A new image of home appears, also without clearly defined forms except for a high, vaulted, beamed ceiling. It is bright and filled with radiance. And ever so faintly, you hear a song softly emerging from rays of light, as if from another world. It is accompanied by melodic strings and notes which pour peace into your soul. You are comforted.

You stand and applaud.

"Dwell in Me, and I will dwell in you."
(John 15:4)

"Jesus answered, If anyone love Me, he will obey My Word
and My Father will love him,
and We will come to him
and make Our home with him."
(John 14:23)

The Bluebird

There is a bluebird. He knows his seasons and has come to build his nest. The iridescent blue on his back catches the morning sun and you are thrilled with his beauty and delighted to see him back again at the farm.

He sits on the fencepost, surveying the pasture as he has done countless times before, waiting for a twitch of grass which could signal "breakfast" to him.

He flies to the bluebird house—the old family homestead for many years, to inspect it for suitability. Are there any spiders? Wasps? Rodents? Snakes? One cannot be too careful when choosing a home.

He sees the gardener. He has seen him many times before and is not fearful. In fact, a favorite perch for food shopping is on top of the gardener's porch roof, especially when the grass has been freshly cut and the birdbath cleaned and filled with fresh water.

You love the bluebird and hope the gardener has prepared for him by clearing out and cleaning the birdhouse from last year's debris and any unwelcome residents.

Apparently he has, for the bluebird sits on top of the house announcing his tenancy and defending it from rival sparrows and swallows.

The female arrives and flies in and out of the house approvingly. They build their nest. They raise their young in their "Home Sweet Home."

"I have prepared for you, My child, by far more carefully than the "gardener," your husband, prepared for the returning bluebirds. All harmful things must be removed and preparations complete before you are able to "nest" again. Please have confidence in your Gardener that I 'do all things well'. I will not disappoint you."

Your loving Father

The Cabin

It looks very dusty and dark inside, this dilapidated, weather-beaten cabin, set back only a few feet from the road you are traveling.

"Why would anyone build here, so close to the road?" you wonder, as you peek through one of the broken windows which face the open front porch.

In the dim light, you see an array of limply drooping cobwebs. The outdoor shutters, each leaning at its own individual angle, are closed on most of the cabin windows, but some are broken here and there, letting in a few timid rays of light. You feel sure that there must be wild creatures here, even underneath the porch and you do not want to meet them. So you step carefully on the old boards, hoping that none will crack and give way beneath you.

"Who might have lived here, and where are they now?" Your mind tumbles with successive questions about the place and its former residents.

"This looks like a spooky scene from a mystery novel," you think, as you wonder whether there might be a dead body or skeleton inside.

Unwilling to be deterred by such scary thoughts, you find a side door, try the rusty latch, and amazingly, it opens with a pained creak. You wander from room to room, ducking cobwebs and almost holding your breath at the thought of discovering a horrific surprise. You feel like Sherlock Holmes, with his magnifying glass hunting for clues.

The furnishings are all gone except for a few, broken chair pieces and against the wall, an old upside down table, which looks like an overturned turtle with legs in the air. Scraps of flower printed wall paper still cling to the walls, aged yellow like an old cheese.

Then you stop. There on the floor, near the front entrance are parts of a very tattered book, torn, and barely legible. Even the author's name is worn off. The book's title reads, _"Time" is a Temporary Commodity_. You hold the delicate volume, pondering the implications of its title. Suddenly the book disintegrates, crumbles, and bits of it fall through your fingers, as if in explanation.

"Once this book was held in the hands of the people who lived here, who sat, spoke together and shared their lives at this table, now broken and upside down. They are all gone. The book is gone. The cabin is silent now, with 'nothing stirring, not even a mouse.'" You turn to leave the lonely desolation, but as you do, you seem to hear the house stir and groan a sigh, as if it knows it has seen its final guest.

You return to the road, which perhaps, then, was only a narrow path, and not a road at all. And you stand there, silent, contemplating what you have seen, held at attention by the stark truth you have witnessed. You reiterate, and carefully enunciate the title of the old book, *"Time" is a Temporary Commodity.*

A sudden gust of wind whips the dust of the road into a tiny whirlwind around your feet, and then hits the cabin, tearing the front porch roof into pieces and depositing its shattered boards, unceremoniously, onto the side yard. As if adding a final exclamation point to the experience.

You continue on your journey, more aware than ever of the fragility of life, of one's brief, measured span of time on this earth, and how precious are the moments we have been given.

And you look up, toward the Eternal One, and pray,

> "Lord, help me to cherish this gift of today. And in it, to love You, and the people whose lives touch mine. Please help me to hold the values of eternity in far greater esteem, than those of fleeting Time."

> *And to your heart comes the assurance, "The eternal God is your refuge, and underneath are the everlasting arms."*

> (Deuteronomy 33:27)

The Long Road

There is a long road ahead of you. You are walking slowly. It is almost time for sunset and you wonder how far you will be able to travel before dark. You are taking methodical, almost military steps, slow, deliberate, and paced evenly. If you would go more slowly, you would get no where. If you increased your pace, you would collapse. So you proceed, step by step, hoping for some divine intervention before either you or the remaining daylight fade.

There is a noise to your side. A familiar friend appears as if from nowhere—surprising and amazing you! You gasp; he smiles and gets in step beside you, matching your pace. It is all too confusing to make any logical sense, so you just accept the comfort of his companionship without the questions which your analytical mind would normally conjure. You are just too tired to think.

"Where are you going," he asks.

"I don't know," you reply. "I once had hopes, but now they seem extremely vague and too distant to define."

"May I carry your provisions?" he offers. You hand him the little bag of tangerines which you have moved from shoulder to shoulder.

As you walk together, he begins to sing. The rhythm of his song is different from the heavy, measured, military cadence of your steps. His melody has a solid beat to it, but incorporates intervals of lighter notes that add life and lilt to the song. His voice is as clear as deep waters of a well. They soothe the thirst of your parched soul.

You begin picking up your steps to match his song, the lyrics of which speak of tumbling waterfalls, luscious, daisy-dotted meadows, with white, fuzzy new-born lambs frolicking in the green, as if the world were made just for play. Just imagining such exuberance stirs the graying, cooling embers of your spirit, and you are thankful.

You still have no answers. But now the traveling seems less like a death march and more like an adventurous trail to a pleasant somewhere.

You round a bend in the road. There in the distance, layered in stark contrast against a cerise and orange sky, is a dusty lavender silhouette of tall roofed house. On either side of it, large trees emerge from a spacious, undulating landscape. The sun, setting just behind the house, seems to frame the scene in golden glory.

You catch your breath, holding it mid-air a few seconds. Then, in a whisper, respond,

"Might that be. . .Could that <u>possibly</u> be…
    HOME?"

"Lo, I am with you always, even unto the end of the age."
(Matthew 28:20)

The River

There is a river with steep banks along most of its course. However, at intervals, there are paths of sandy dirt which go down to the water where one may access the river. They are partially grown over, but those who know where they are can scramble down to the water's edge in a few seconds.

You are there, having scooted down the slope, shoes in hand, and are now eager to feel the cool flow over your tired and dusty feet. There is a new moon rising. You can see it through the trees even though it is not quite dark.

"How long shall I stay by the river?" you wonder. Darkness and snakes are not a girl's friend.

"But the River is my friend," you declare. "It is moving forward as I am, although it does not know its destination any more than I do. Its forward movement continues and on its journey it carries travelers to their destinations; it provides food and pleasure for the fishermen and refreshment for one such as I who needs cool waters and a friend."

"I want to be like the River," you say to your heart. "I want to keep moving forward and helping people along their journeys. I want to help those in need."

You look up at the new moon which appears to be smiling at you. You look past the new moon to the One you trust, and He is smiling as well. And you turn your wish into a prayer; "Lord, may I be like my River friend, and before I reach my final destination—that boundless, eternal sea, may I help, nourish and refresh those who come my way."

The new moon's smile seems to broaden. A beam of its light catches a small rippling wave in the river, and the river sparkles and splashes, in approval.
You climb up the river bank, put on your shoes and hurry down the road to find shelter before dark.

The Missed Turn

"Oh how I wish I could know the schedule for tomorrow," you exclaim as you step onto the road this morning. "Then I would know how far I must travel today, and if there is time for a short nap when the sun is high. Or if I need to keep up my pace to make proper progress."

"Tomorrow might even hold my long awaited 'surprise'—the good thing, the good place I am pursuing." Your imagination goes there, surveying possibilities which may exist.

On the side of the road, you see a little frog who lies very flat and very dead. Squashed. You don't like frogs, but this one looked so pitifully dead, you could not help but speak condolences. "I'm sorry you did not make it to your 'tomorrow', Frog. You might have found a lily pad with a she-frog waiting for you, had you not met your untimely end."
You continue your consistent rhythm of steps, walking straight ahead, and looking intently as far as possible at the road ahead of you. This seems like a never ending journey, "but perhaps tomorrow," you think, "I'll get a glimpse of where I am heading." Again, your imagination visits your destination.

You miss a turn. It was only a small opening between the high bushes on either side of the road. And the shadows cast by the early sun` darkened the narrow trail. You pass by it, unaware.

The trail leads away from the road you are traveling, through a meadow, beside a pond, around a hill, and then back again to join your familiar road.

You could have spent the day there, happily engaged in watching the young fawns coming to drink at the pond; listening to the many song birds who have so much to sing about in this lovely place. You missed the fragrances of the flowers blooming along the banks of the pond (probably the intended destination of the frog!) And you did not see the colorful congregation of water lilies, which would have inspired you to paint again.

You missed seeing the small New England "cape" on the hill, overlooking the pond. It looks exactly like the one you see in your dreams. Who knows what welcome you might have received there?

But the "Tomorrow" in your mind was so large that it blocked your vision of "Today." You were so pre-occupied with what <u>will</u> or <u>could be</u>, that you missed what <u>is.</u>
So you missed the turn. And the delightful day of respite and pleasure I had planned for you.

I'm sorry, child. Please tune in more closely to My voice and My heart's desire for each of your "todays." I would not have you miss any other good gifts from your loving Father.

The Tree

You think it is silly, but you <u>really</u> want to climb that tree! It stands a few yards off the side of the road yet it draws you with its inviting shade and you see its sequence of limbs which makes it <u>perfect</u> for climbing. Some things one never forgets. Now, however, the thought of climbing it seems preposterous. You haven't climbed a tree in many decades and now, with your weakness, you wonder if you are capable at all. Yet no one is around, no one is looking, so you think, "Why not try?"

You hurry off the path to the tree and reach up to the lowest limb of the tree, thinking, "This is crazy. Why am I doing this?"

The child in you answers, "Why not?"

So you try. You lift yourself up with both arms, holding fast to the lowest limb and reaching for the next higher one. Then with do or die effort, you hoist yourself up, reach for the next higher limb, and then stand up, having conquered your Everest.

In the process, you've scratched your knee on the rough grey bark, but you hardly notice, so great is your amazement that you made it. You, at your age, could still climb a tree! This is fun!

Your arms ache at the exertion, but you laugh at yourself. You look at the ground below, and with sincere questioning, ask, "Now—how shall I get down?"
Reverting to childhood instinct, you land, hitting the ground hard, but happy.

And to my heart, God spoke. "You have forgotten much of how it feels to be a child, to enjoy the "Why nots?" of an adventure."

"So aging robs many of that child-like spirit which does not overly calculate and dwell on all that could go wrong, and thus draws back, in fear, from all risks."

"I lead with wisdom; not fear. I detest the stale. I rotted the manna quickly to keep My people from putting their confidence in their stored <u>Reserve</u> (even of bread of heaven!), rather than in their <u>Relationship</u> with Me. Only in that relationship is there true security."

"I will lead you carefully; never foolishly. But I will not exempt from the equation, what <u>I can do</u>, or what <u>we</u> can do together!

"Nor should you. So listen carefully to My Spirit's direction to your heart. He may lead you to save a "reserve" or to spend it; to play it safe, and <u>not</u> climb a tree, or give it a try and see just how far you can get!

"You might even have made it to the next limb higher!"

Your playful Father,
God

"In Your presence there is fullness of joy;
at Your right hand there are pleasures forevermore."
(Psalm 16:11)

The Sun

The countryside where you are traveling today is open and wide, with tall grasses waving in the summer breeze as if an invisible hand were stroking them. Their motion reminds you of ocean waves being lifted, then soothed by the winds. How you long to see the ocean again! You feel <u>very</u> far "inland." Too, too far away from that natural beauty which stirs your imagination and artistry.

You feel like lying down to rest, so you wander off your path into the grassy field to find a safe and unobtrusive spot. You pile some of the grasses together to make a pillow and lie down, hidden from sight by a wall of green around you.

Watching the clouds above you, traveling to their "somewhere," makes you wish you could be light as a leaf and be blown along with them. You'd like to see what they see from their higher elevation and perspective.

"Perhaps if I just follow the clouds, I'll get to my "somewhere," you muse in playful thought. "At least I could see the road ahead."

Suddenly thunder rumbles in the distance like an angry god clearing his throat. The storm moves closer and huge raindrops pelt the ground, giving way to a barrage of hailstones which flatten the once waving grass, narrowly missing your hidden resting place.

At last, quiet returns. But you are afraid. You feel vulnerable and you quiver with insecurity. You look up to see the sun breaking through the bank of dark, churning clouds racing toward their next appointment.

"I cannot follow the clouds," you reason. "They can turn into storms! I cannot hide in tall grass, for hail can level it instantly."

The sun emerges fully from its hiding place behind the clouds and shines on you in assurance. It was there and shining when the waving grasses beckoned you. It was there, hidden, as you thought you had been, throughout the storm. It was not moved or lessened by the storm.

And it will continue to shine, as scheduled by its Maker, so long as your days shall last.

You are comforted. You throw a kiss at the sun; pray a prayer to its Maker, and continue on your journey.

A sunny yellow butterfly swoops just before you on your path.

"While the earth remains, seedtime and harvest,. . .day and night shall not cease."
(Genesis 8:22)

The Cat

As you journey today, your memory travels back to farm times and the menagerie of animals you have loved, patted, birthed and found companionship in their company. You smile, remembering their antics. There is yellow lab, Emily, your "Hallelujah" dog who, when she heard your car approaching the driveway, would sit back on her haunches, raise both forelegs high to the sky, as if rejoicing, "Hallelujah, you are home!"

You remember your first he-goat, Sweet Pepper, born in your garage with his sister, Snowflake. Pepper was white with black and grey spots and had an overbite which made him look as if he needed braces. Whenever you would go into the pasture, he would come running to walk with you. And when you would sit down on a granite boulder to rest, Pepper would lie down, positioning himself just behind your back so that you could lean back and rest on his warm frame.

And then there was grey, fluffy, Maine coon cat, Lucy. From where ever she was in the yard, as soon as you came out of the house to take a walk in the woods, she would run to you. You would pick her up and carry her on your shoulder, scratching her back for the entire walk.

Now they are gone, and how you grieved their passing. But now you smile as you remember them, and others you hold in your animal loving heart.

Then, with a leap, there emerges from the bushes on the roadside, a stately, grey tiger cat with tail held high. He looks quite regal, actually. He greets you as if you were an old acquaintance and falls into step beside you, looking at you and then at the road ahead as if he knows the road better than you do. You don't doubt it, thinking of a cat's nine lives.

You like him and start conversation as if he could understand. "Hello, Cat Friend! I'm glad to have you walk with me. Do you have any suggestions as to any <u>short</u> <u>cuts</u> to where ever we are going?"

He stops at once and looks at you. Then he begins rolling playfully in the dust of the road, then darting back and forth on it, and rolling again. He exerts much more energy at play than if he just walked straight ahead! Then he jumps to the side of the road, through the bushes, and returns, as if inviting you to come with him. You follow and find a little brook running fresh and clear. You both lean down and lap of its waters. Nearby, he locates a large pine cone and flips it out into the narrow road where he tumbles and plays with it, batting it, chasing and catching it, again and again, as if it were his mouse catch of the day.

You watch him, happily enjoying his "now" and being more concerned with the moment, rather than forward movement. Or, on getting to where ever he is going. He seems to be more invested in the <u>present</u> than in the <u>potential</u> or the <u>possible</u>.

And you wonder if you have not missed something BIG!

You wonder, "Are there 'now' moments I have overlooked, in my 'leap-frog' mentality, to get where I am going? Have I thought too much about the situations and possibilities of the future, and my responsibilities in getting there—and so have missed the sweet pleasure of savoring the present moment? Have I lost the joy of the 'now?'"

You turn to your cat friend, and admit, "I'm glad, Cat Friend that you can play and enjoy the moments of your journey, but I'll have to say, rolling in the dust does <u>not</u> appeal to me."

With that, the cat swats his pine cone a few feet in front of you.

"Just watch!" you say to him. You back up, laugh, poise yourself like a soccer player for a moment…and then run and kick that pine cone right out of sight!

Thanks, Cat!

The Flower

As you travel today you spot something bright yellow beside the road ahead of you. You move closer. "Oh, it's only a dandelion." you observe, "And there are many, many of them scattered on the hillside."

But it is a cheery color, in contrast to the grey day, so you pick it up and look at it more closely. You are amazed at its intricacies and its masterful design. You pick another, this one "going to seed" and touch the soft, delicate, fluffy globe, ready to launch on its seed distribution assignment. As you have done many times as a child, you blow on it and watch it almost explode in all directions, each seed flying away, happily headed for its own destiny and destination.

In your concentration, you realize that you have stepped on some of the dandelions on the ground.

"Oh, I'm sorry. I didn't mean to step on your pretty faces!" you exclaim. But somehow, they seem to recover in record time. You pick another and hold it in your hand, with new respect.

"Little Dandelion," you say. "I apologize for calling you 'just' a dandelion, and considering you as <u>only</u> a weed, and not a <u>real</u> flower at all! But you are who God made you to be! You bring the world color and beauty, and although I've never tasted your petals or leaves or made tea from your roots, I do recall that one may do so and be nourished!"

"You do not require man's cultivation, attention, or approval. You do not appear in great paintings in museums, or in centerpiece arrangements on dining room tables. Yet you continue, undeterred and undiminished to be all that your Maker intended."

"Thank you, lovely Dandelion Flower! May I be as free and resilient as you! May I bloom and not be dismayed or reduced in effectiveness by lack of man's approval or applause. Or by comparison with other flowers esteemed more highly, which he chooses as centerpieces for his tables. And may I recover and keep blooming, even if someone steps in my face!"

You drape the dandelion over your ear in decoration, whistle a happy tune, and continue on your journey, a little freer in your heart.

The Girl and the Dog

The road bends, turning toward the right. To the left, there is an intersection where another road joins the one you are traveling. From it, coming toward you, you see a young girl, about your age carrying a small bundle. She too, appears to be set on a journey. You wait until she is within hearing distance and call out, "Hello. Are you traveling, as I am?"

The Girl answers, "Yes, although I'm not sure of where I am going!"

Knowing that familiar, uncomfortable feeling, you reply, "Nor do I! Perhaps we might be going to the same place!"

"Perhaps," she responds. "I only know I am headed somewhere that is good — difficult to find — but my heart tells me that I must go there."

You introduce yourselves and stand silent a few moments, considering options. Suddenly, from the direction the Girl had just come, a huge dog bounds toward the two of you. He wags his tail furiously, like a windshield wiper in a heavy rain storm. His whole body wags, articulating wildly, as if his front and back parts were only lightly hinged together.

He is massive. His long yellow hair which is full of dust, flips and flops as he greets you with the slobbery, exuberant enthusiasm of which only dogs are capable. You girls squeal and laugh at a pitch of which only girls are capable.

"Could we travel together?" You both ask the question almost simultaneously. And then you laugh again, both knowing the answer. The Dog wags himself all over again, knowing that he is part of the trio. He will not be denied.

It is pleasant, but a bit awkward at first, not knowing anything about your new traveling companion. But gradually you begin asking questions about the other's life.

You discover that the Girl has inner wounds, many of them; yet she seems genuinely concerned about your hurts. She begins to relate to you some of her adventures and the lessons she has learned from the One she loves and trusts. The One who speaks to her heart and is telling her to journey bravely toward what He has planned for her.

The stories of her woundings touch your heart, and you share with her some of the lessons you have learned in your travels. You both know that the same One is leading each of you.

The Dog prances between you as you walk, tossing his head from side to side, as he enjoys pats and scratches from your hand, and then from the Girl's. He feels he has reached heaven, already!

Your heart feels lighter. You find yourself thinking about your friend's hurts and needs, and you forget your own.

Your focus is now more outward—less inward toward yourself, and that feels "good."

A yellow butterfly crosses the road just in front of you, dipping and tipping its wings as if in cheerful greeting. He continues his flight in front of you.

You are at peace, and content.

This is a "good" day.

"And God said, 'It is not good that man should be alone...'"
(Genesis 2:18)

The House

"Banana yellow," you say. "That is how I would describe the color of this house—soft, yet with enough strength of color to say, 'I am definitely a yellow house!'"

You have just "happened" on this house as you have journeyed today, alone again. The Girl and the Dog took another road which she was sure was the "right" one for her. So with kind well wishes you parted and have not traveled long today before encountering this story book house. It has drawn your attention like a powerful magnet. Its classic, white picket fence circles the front yard as if embracing the colorful flower beds. Over the side gate, there is a sturdy arched arbor holding hundreds of morning glories up to face the sun. Its lattice work, entwined with the cool blues of the flowers and greens of the leaves invites you to stand beneath it out of the sun. A yellow butterfly swoops and loops through the arbor, contrasting vividly to the deep sky blues of the morning glories.

On the front porch of the house there is a welcoming porch swing, white, matching the house trim, and it all looks as if it must have appeared magically, like a "poof" from Aladdin's lamp.

You were just passing by en route to your "somewhere," but this house halts you, and any desire to go one step further. Its charm is more than your fanciful imagination could have pictured. But is it real? You touch the flowers and feel their life. But who lives here?

You want to know with everything in you but you are a bit afraid to find out. That person and this place may be quite different, and you still feel too weak to encounter rebuff.

But you must know. You open the white gate beneath the arbor and step carefully on each stone leading to the front steps, the porch and the front door which is painted a sea-side blue.

You knock, three gentle taps. The heavy wrought iron, antique knocker feels solid and sure in your hands, and you wonder about all the people through all the years who have held this knocker, asking for entrance.

You hear footsteps and you hold your breath. You step backward a bit as the door opens.

There, in rough but neat jeans and a bright plaid shirt stands your father. You remember him only from photographs, for he died when you were two years old. But he looks exactly the same as he did in the photograph of him which you framed and hung on your bedroom wall. In it he is holding you as an infant, in his arms. You were told that you called him, "Daddy Boy," and that he loved you very much.

Of course he knows you immediately, but is quietly respectful of your topsy-turvy emotions and tumbling thoughts. Amazement, confusion and wild questions race with hilarious ecstasy around and around in your mind.

"Welcome home, my Daughter." He extends his arms toward you to embrace you and you cannot get within those arms fast enough. Time stand still. You feel the love that you missed and longed for most of your life.

You are both weeping and laughing in a rhapsody of joyful reunion. Slowly he turns and says, "Come and see the view from the back porch windows."

You enter the room. Large panes of windows climb the high wall and extend several feet into the ceiling, allowing you to view the clear blue sky above you. Stretching away from the house is a lush green meadow, garnished with dewdrops which appear as emeralds as they are touched by the filtered sunlight. Ancient oak trees shade the meadow, and in the distance, but not so far away, is the opalescent turquoise sea!

<u>The turquoise sea!</u>

You and your father kick off your shoes, and run toward it, together.

The Turquoise Sea

The morning sun is peeking around the edges of the window shades as you awaken in the bedroom which your father prepared for you. He told you that he knew you were coming and he wanted it to be pretty and ready for you.

Its walls, like the house are a soft yellow with white, wide crown molding and trim. It windows are topped with deep valances of Battenburg lace (your favorite.) The upholstery covering the cushioned chaise lounge and the many fluffy pillows around the room is country French chintz. The design is composed of large voluptuous cabbage roses, in white and shades of pink against a sunny yellow background, with a touch of blue cornflowers as accent.

The bedspread is also white and hand quilted into patterns which look like the rippled contours of wet sand, sculptured by incoming waves caressing the shore. The bed looks exactly like your grandmother's ("Dearie")—a high, four posted, spool bed, a "Jenny Lind" antique. You drop your feet off the side of the bed into the deep pile, rose carpet which matches the deepest pink in the roses. You wiggle your toes and it welcomes you with its soft texture.

"What more would a girl like me ever want?" you sigh in sweet contentment. But as you lift the shade, you see that "more"— a breath taking view of the turquoise sea and its border of whitest sand. "This is unbelievable! It is <u>way</u> over the top!" you exclaim in amazement.

"And how did I get here?" you wonder, again, astounded at the seemingly accidental, unscripted events, and the many turns and twists of your dusty road to "somewhere."

Still pondering these thoughts, you notice a door you had not seen when you arrived yesterday. All the doors in the house are painted white and are made of heavy, solid wood, with rectangular panels in the "Cross and Bible" design. You like the doorknob. It is heavy, solid, antique brass. You turn it, and the door opens into a large studio, radiant with light, with easel, canvas and paints already set in place, waiting for an artist's hand.

French doors and almost to the floor windows reveal the view. Again, it is the turquoise sea, only from this angle you can see high waves energetically hitting a tall, rocky ledge and the surrounding boulders.

"Is this the coast of Maine? Or is this Heaven? Where am I?" You almost shout your questions.

The Answers

In the blue and white kitchen nearby, from which wafts the fragrances of fresh coffee and bacon, your father hears you as you shout the questions which are almost too large to utter. "Is this the Maine coast? Is this Heaven? Where am I anyway?" You sound desperate to know.

"Neither!" your father answers. "You are not in Maine, nor in Heaven, but here with me, in your father's house!"

You dress quickly and come to sit across from him at the round marble top table. He serves you very strong coffee, hoping it helps you understand more clearly what he has to explain to you.

"Here in my house, you feel secure in my love, and safe in your earthly father's care. Here you are free to explore and fulfill you callings and destiny. This, my child, is <u>your here and now.</u> What you are experiencing here, now, is the way you can live the rest of your days on earth—safe and secure in your <u>Heavenly Father's</u> love, even more than you are in mine."

"No, Heaven is not yet. It lies just over the horizon, the tall mountainous region just beyond the turquoise sea. The sea is alive with the Spirit and just as the sea draws all the streams of earth into itself, so the Holy Spirit draws mankind to come to the eternal waters of life, to come as close to the sea as possible and merge one's life into its waters."

"Here, near the sea, the winds bring heaven's thoughts and ideas which can be heard and understood, and even its music, which one hears when all is still. The sea conveys the energies and enthusiasms of Heaven—and brings <u>The Presence</u>—which is as close to heaven as earth can get."

"Near the sea, in the atmosphere of The Presence is a place available to all. No matter what one's geographic location, whatever one's specific longitude or latitude on earth's grid, <u>to everyone</u>, this sublime place is accessible in the very real spirit realm. To enter it requires a journey, sacrifice, and a passionate desire for Him, above all else."

"So, my Daughter, as you have traveled toward the turquoise sea, you have been drawn toward The Presence of God. The dusty road has led you here, and along the way you have been liberated from many patterns of thought which have hindered your freedom. Some of the lessons have been directed to the little girl in you; others, to the adult in you, healing you and freeing you. Like a butterfly emerging from a dark cocoon, you are now ready for "life on wings."

"Thank you, Father," you express with heartfelt gratitude.

You finish your coffee in silence, then walk into the brightness of your new studio and begin to paint. As so often happens, you "lose yourself" and all track of time as you work, happily, arranging colors, forms and designs and breathing deeply of the breezes from the sea.

Abruptly, the telephone rings. You are startled into sudden and stark "reality."

You put your paint brush down, answer the phone, and hear a recorded message saying, "This is the office of Florida Cancer Specialists, calling to remind you of your appointment on. . . . ." Her voice fades as she speaks the date and time. Dazed, you push the requested key on the telephone, to confirm your appointment, and then hold to your easel to steady yourself. You look around at your studio, a tiny space set in the corner of the small bedroom which was your husband's before he moved to Assisted Living.

"Where is my bright studio with its view to the sea? What <u>was</u> all of that?" Your thoughts are spinning; your body is aching.

You sit down on the edge of the hospital bed, which had been your husband's. You put your head in your hands, trying to make sense out of all the episodes of the journey. They all seemed so real, so <u>very</u> real!

At long last you conclude, "I do not understand what I have just experienced. It was wonderfully confusing. I do know that many people have actually visited heaven, come back and have written books about their experiences."

"But, no, I did not visit Heaven. But perhaps. . . .just maybe,

Heaven visited me."

As you recall the exquisite joys of your father's house, and the bliss of nearness to the sea, an intense longing rises in you to get as close to Heaven as earth can get—as close to The Presence—the Presence of the Living God—as humanly possible! You yearn to hear the sounds of heaven, to walk in its wisdom, to fully experience the Father's love, to revel in the companionship of Jesus, to splash in the exhilarating waters of the Spirit and to know the freedom "to be" which only He can bring.

You turn that longing into a prayer, that this desire—to live in The Presence of God—might be your consuming passion and priority for the rest of your days.

You pick up your paint brush to resume your work, and mix a shade of the brightest turquoise possible.

As you do, a yellow butterfly floats past your window.

To the Curious Reader

If you are curious, you may be wondering, "What is fact and what is fiction here? What is "real earth" statistic, and what is imaginative allegory?

To answer, I suggest that you consider this writing as a tossed salad—comprised of pieces of one thing, and parts of another, hopefully blending together into something edible and nourishing.

Yes, indeed, there are many actual, literal places and people pictured here, one of which is the New Hampshire farm with its literal zip code of 03440. The animals there, their names and antics were all "real" in earth terms. Even the bluebirds—the zip code of whose bird house was also 03440!

And yes, we have recently moved to Florida, to be near our daughter, Pam and her family. And here, temporarily, we are renting part of a house. And yes, my husband, Burt has been afflicted with Parkinson's disease for thirteen years, and now has moved to an assisted living facility. That is literal.

As is the all-too-true "fact" that I am being treated at The Florida Cancer Specialists, Sarasota, Florida, for Stage Four lung cancer, although I have never smoked a cigarette! (However, we have not heard the last of this story!)

As to the people I have mentioned: My friend, Beverly Bakke lives in Spofford, NH; master painter, Peter Granucci, lives in Gilsum, New Hampshire; my biological father, George Austin Wilson, lives in Heaven, having died when I was two years old. And yes, I was told that I called him, "Daddy-Boy" and that he loved me very much.

But I will tell you this: When I was writing the piece called "The House" and was "there" on the front porch, having knocked on the front door and waiting. Hearing footsteps, and wondering, a bit afraid of who might open the door—I did not have a <u>clue</u> as to <u>who</u> that might be! I was holding my breath, literally, listening for the next sentence.

I had no more idea of how the script would read than did you, the reader. And then the next words came to my mind. "There in rough but clean jeans, in a bright plaid shirt, stands your father." I wept—literally—which I did throughout our "reunion" but which I saw only in my mind's eye. But to my heart, it felt <u>very</u> "real."

So, the story line of this collection of vignettes, I believe has been "given." That is, I did not begin with an idea, or a story to tell, and then proceed to design how to develop it and make it readable, and hopefully, helpful to others.

No, it began in morning devotions, when I read, pray and journal the thoughts that come, thoughts that instruct, correct and comfort me. That is when I "connect" with God. I take very literally His words when He promised, "Call unto Me and I will answer you and show you great and mighty things which you do not know." (Jeremiah 33:3) I am not seeking the "great and mighty" but surely, I am looking to Him to "<u>answer</u>!" To communicate with me, as father to his child.

My friend, Beverly called, telling me of her "vision" of me as a sad little girl, kicking a can down a dusty road. And very soon afterward, and continuing each day for many weeks, the words and ideas came which form this collection. At first, it might be only the title and the introductory sentence. Then as I would write, the flow would come, including thoughts, visuals, and understandings which were as fresh to me as manna. Of course, I had to do my part. This was no dictation. I had to incorporate His words into descriptions of what I was seeing and hearing. And explain what I saw as "pictures," putting them into words, which I hoped would adequately convey the images. I heard no audible "voice;" I had no "out-of-the-body" experience. I only listened to God's Spirit.

What I "heard" certainly holds no "authority" for anyone's "doctrine," and perhaps will not be pertinent to anyone's life but my own. But I do hope that these writings will brush the dust off of a few tired feet, and encourage a few travelers on their journey.

So, enjoy this tossed salad of fact and fantasy, specific literals combined with the imaginative and the allegorical.

But is not the purpose of allegory to reveal truth in symbolic form?

And is not <u>truth</u>, that which we all seek?

Our son, Stephen asked me, "Mom, did you <u>really</u> climb that tree?
I told him the answer, but I will keep <u>you</u> guessing. . .

Thank you for taking the time to journey with me.

Sincerely,

Jane W. Lauber

A Sampling of Paintings and Poems

of

Land, Sea, and Scripture

from the "Caterpillar" years

"You, O Lord, have made me glad by Your works,
at the works of Your hands
I sing for joy."

(Psalm 92:4)

Although the subjects of my paintings and poetry
are not all "religious," I make no distinction between the
secular and the sacred.
To me, it is all sacred.
Therefore my work is my joyful response, my sincere worship
to God, the Creator.

I love the beauty of the earth, the color and drama of sea and sky,
the interplay of light and darkness.
I believe that "all nature sings"
and I pray that my poems and paintings
might echo those songs
for the glory of God.

Contents, Part II

LAND

As a Lover Courts	56
Painting # 1, The Rose	57
The Day Lily	58
Painting # 2, "Consider the Lilies"	59
Painting # 3, The Gold Lily	60
Painting # 4, The Red Lily	61
Lord of Lilacs	62
Painting # 5, Lilacs by the Window	63
Lilacs, Butterfly and Bee	64
Reversed Decree	65
The Mint Bed	66
Painting # 6, Gardens by the Sea	67
Dearie's Daisies	68
Painting # 7, My New Hampshire Garden	69
To A Bumblebee	70
Painting # 8, Mt. Monadnock in Spring	51
Spring Fashion Show (same page)	71
His Lamb am I	72
The Monarch (essay)	73
The Woodland Concert	74
Paintings # 9 and 10, Waterfalls	75
Autumn Celebration	76
Grande Finale (same page)	76
Painting # 11, Fall Stream	77
Late Winter Fog	78
Painting # 12, There is a River	79
Apology	80

SEA

Waters' Edge 83
Painting # 13, Lupine on the Maine Coast 84
Preference (same page) 84
Dinner Guest 85
Fine Feathered Friend 86
Winter Shore 87
Drops of Distinction 88
Sunrise with Sanderlings 89
Painting # 14, Sunrise 90
Sunrise Surprise (same page) 90
Resistance 91
Simon Says 93
Painting # 15, Storm at Sea 92
Invitation 95
Painting # 16, The Blue Sea 96
Today 97

SCRIPTURE

Psalm 139:7-10 100
"Where Shall I Flee?" 101
Breath of Beauty 102
Painting # 18, "Alpha and Omega" I, *(Revelation 1:11)* 103
Painting # 19, "Alpha and Omega" II, *(Colossians 1:15-17)* 104
Painting # 20, "I Am the Alpha and Omega" 105
Close Call 106
Painting # 21, Look Up! 107
Noah's Ark (same page) 107
The Soldier 108
Painting # 22, For Me 109
Ram in the Thicket 110
Painting # 23, The Lamb, Slain 111
Broken Bread 112
Painting # 24, Crown of Thorns 113
The Thorn (same page) 113
Painting # 25, "He is Risen!" 114
Painting # 26, "I AM the Resurrection and the Life" 115
The Stones Cry Out 116

Painting # 27, Waiting for the Trumpet 117
The Stained Glass Window 118
Painting # 28, "Death is Swallowed Up in Victory" 119
Two Gateways, Sealed and Shut 120
Painting # 29, Sealed and Shut 121
Painting # 30, The River Flows 122
Hosanna! (same page) 122
Painting # 31, "Come to the Throne" 123
Performing in the Presence 124
Painting # 32, "Holy, Holy, Holy" 125
Painting # 33 Sailing Toward the City 127
First Love, Painting #34, (yellow butterfly, detail from cover) 129

LAND

As a Lover Courts

As a lover courts
the one his heart desires,
   with whispered tenderness, and gifts of love—
      sweet perfumed flowers,
      melodies and jewels—
         hoping to attract, convince of his intent
         to have, to hold forever.

So God bestows bouquets
even fields of daffodils, white perfumed lilies
   and the rose;
      bright gifts of sunsets, songs of birds
      and sparkling diamonds on the snow.

"Courting" human hearts—expressing His!
And whispering, "I AM! I LOVE YOU!
   YOU are My heart's desire!
   I want you as My OWN—
      Forever—"

The Rose

The Day Lily

Open but a day—One note to play—
One note of beauty sounded—that is all.

While other notes of other blossoms play in symphony—
Continuing for days, or weeks, or more.

One note—then gone.

But oh, that note!
And oh, that day, in which it spends its glory!

Unfurling bright pure petals, it opens doors for bees and birds
To share its fragrant life.

So, LORD—may I, like lily with one note to play
Fill precious moments of *this* day
With all the beauty You designed as mine.

With festive, fragrant heart—as open door
Through which Your glory—bright and pure, may shine.

*"This is the day which the Lord has made;
we will rejoice and be glad in it."*

(Psalm 118:24)

"Consider the Lilies"

The Gold Lily

The Red Lily

Lord of Lilacs

Lord of lavender,
Lord of lilacs.,
    Lover of my soul—

Lord of primrose,
Lord of mountain pinks,
    Lord of passion,

Breathe on me and be
Loved and Lover of my soul.

With scent of apple blossoms
In honeysuckle nectar,
    Pour on me Your fragrant oils of Spring—

And I will pour on You,
Upon Your feet, as Mary did
My oils, extracted from crushed petals of my heart.

Upon Your tired and dusty feet
    Which bore the dirt of earth,
        Which walked on waves—but then
            Were pierced with iron;

    But when—someday—upon the Mount are placed,
    Those feet will split the earth!
    Its kingdoms overturn!

Upon those feet I pour
That perfumed essence of my soul,
    With hope of Spring.

Lord of the Lovely,
Lord of Lilacs,
Breathe and pour on me.

Lilacs by the Window

As I was preparing dinner, one late afternoon of Spring in New Hampshire, just outside my window was an unlikely couple going "out" for dinner.

Lilacs, Butterfly and Bee—

This moment is so fragile, Lord—
Like fragrance of the lilac blooms—
Like brief encounters of a butterfly and bee,
Together dining in the evening light.

Though fragrance fades,
And lilacs fall,
Bright butterflies and bees pass by—
They leave their call
For praise eternal,
In my soul!

Reversed Decree

Wordsworth's daffodils, Degas' chrysanthemums,
Sunflowers by Van Gogh, and Shakespeare's rose
Through art, received expanded scope,
Extended life —

Death's verdict countermanded
By an artist's hand!

And I, as they, condemned to life's brief bloom,
Will breathe the freshness of immortal air,
Explore terrains of joy unmapped on human charts —

Death's verdict countermanded
By a Savior's hand!

The Mint Bed

Mint's intent—to cover earth—
Its lengthy longitude and girth—
Assigned but bit part in the play,
It nabs the leading role away!

Though just an herb, for tea or such
As needs a spice or garnish touch. . .
As band barbarian invades
A hapless hamlet, mint parades
O'er daisies, phlox, petunias, kale—
Whatever else cannot prevail
Against the conquering minty horde.

I'll take my trusty trowel-sword
And STOP expansionist assault!
At *my* set limit, mint must halt!

Dear Lord, may no activity
However fine a spice it be—
Take over. Spoil Your Plan's intent—
And turn my life
To mass of mint!

Gardens By the Sea

My grandmother, Lucile Sharp, was called "Dearie" by all of our family. She was the most influential person in my young life. As an artist, her love of nature and painting inspired me. As a warm, cheerful, " free-spirit" activist, she enlarged my vision. And as a Scripture-loving and Scripture-living Believer, she kept my sights on the eternal.

As I transplanted some of Dearie's flowers from her Mississippi garden to my New Hampshire garden, I wrote these words:

Dearie's Daisies

**Her clematis blooms at my window
   Dearie's daisies by my door.
      Here in blustery, cold New England,
         Southern flowers find rapport
            Side by side with northern blossoms.**

**Yet, deeper rooted in my heart
   Are memories of Dearie's nurture,
      Dearie's spirit, Dearie's art.**

**Lord—perhaps up there in Glory—
   You might suggest, before I come
      To take up Heaven's residence—**

She plant some daisies by my door.

My New Hampshire Garden

To A Bumblebee

Your dining elegance exceeds our best décor—
A foxglove blossom corridor through which you stroll.
Past pearlized pinks, in hanging tapestries—-
On carpets spread with lavender and white designs—
Until you reach the golden cup from which you drink.

Then on you fly—
To bright Sweet William's lively pub—
Then on from there to Towered Lupine's lavish fare!~
What beauty God prepared for thee—
An ordinary Bumblebee.

Spring Fashion Show

Posing fashion models wear
Designers' new "sensations"—-
They pivot, turn—-Awards declare
The *best* of Spring's creations.

The earth—-all dressed in new attire
Is turning on its axis
For all its viewers to admire—
But *this* one's just for *practice!*

"I saw a new heaven and a new earth,
for the first heaven and the first earth
were passed away."

(Revelation 21:1)

One sunny Spring morning in New Hampshire, as I was driving on our road to town, an exquisite scene made me stop the car. In the pasture beside an antique New England "cape," about a dozen newly born, fluffy white lambs were frolicking among a profusion, at least hundreds, of bright yellow daffodils. The lambs were leaping from boulder to boulder, and then, after a while, would sit against the warm stones to rest. It became a magical memory. And a poem.

His Lamb Am I

His Lamb am I—
Though weak and helpless, formed to be His Own—
To play in pastures dressed in daffodils
As Spring arrives—
Where granite boulders, basking in the sun's warm rays
Rest beside me in my pastures green.

I feel His arms, holding, loving my clumsy, fearful frame;
I know His hand, His oil upon my head.
I hear His voice,
Calling, leading, corralling me to safety.

And sense, though I am just a lamb, (and "dumb")
Such care will follow me, as well as lead
Through weary, rocky ways
Of dangers' dark uncertainties,
Through storms and murky mists
Where sight is lost—

Until, through pasture gates of Heavenly terrain,
I come, and dance with daffodils,
And know, eternally,
His Lamb am I.

(Another "magical" memory)
The Monarch

It is an early morning of late August in New Hampshire. The cool, crisp air makes my fleece robe feel cozy as I sit on the porch beside my "fresh-washed" garden. The lingering droplets of last night's rain sparkle like jewels on the bright yellow chrysanthemums, and hot pink impatiens, boldly displaying their festive dress. A ruby-throated humming bird in his iridescent green top coat, secures his "fly-through" breakfast from a purple petunia, hanging less than a yard from me. While a wren dressed in his far more conservative business-brown, dances on my picket fence. Late summer beauty is heady stuff!

In the background, our maple tree adds her notes of color with intense red leaves appearing on the tips of her limbs, signaling change of the seasons. Nature does her "Transitions" so very well. I do not. Somehow my heart holds far too tightly to the near and dear, and I do not want to let them go! I don't even want to let my flowers go, as Fall and frost arrive.

But the leaves are turning on the maple, and also in the book of our lives; a change of seasons is imminent. Heartless Parkinson's disease has robbed Burt of his ability to maintain this property which we love so dearly. We know we must leave. But I am not handling it well, and am bombarded with questions and fears about what the future might bring. Sadness, as thick fog, seems to settle over my garden, obscuring its beauty.

Suddenly, "Heaven to the rescue!" Onto center stage in my garden flies a majestic yellow-orange Monarch butterfly, who touches down gently upon a yellow-orange Black-eyed Susan. The sun spot-lights his dramatic appearance. As I contemplated his beauty; and the daring and dangers of his perilous life-cycle, I feel challenged and instructed.
"The Monarch dwells on the beautiful. He seeks and savors the nectar of today, and flies on, with wings unencumbered, bearing no burdens, but only the brushstrokes of the design of God."

                              Lord, may I do the same.

The Woodland Concert

Within a green and sunlight-sequined wood
I heard a symphony, and running, found
A waterfall, within a mountain gorge
Where rocky walls enclosed a concert hall.

The notes and melodies were being spilled
In sweet profusion over multi-tiers;
The stops and rests, contributed expertly
By silent pools, at proper intervals.

I joined the main floor audience of stones,
And sat beside a bulky dowager
Whose dress was velvet, of a mossy green—
A tuft of fern adorned her weathered head.

The rows in front contained a concert crowd
Of Elegants—pyrite and mica-flecked—
Bejeweled and glittering for the occasion—
Resplendent in their softly varied hues.

In granite balconies which rimmed the hall,
Stood hemlock, spruce, and birch, in greens and golds—
And leaning over, not to miss a note,
They murmured approbation of the score.

I listened through the day, then quietly left—
But still the symphony plays on and on.
Continuing throughout the scheduled season,
'Til Winter lowers his crisp and brisk baton.

Waterfalls

75

Autumn Celebration

Autumn's Celebration—
Astounding every eye—
Leaves in loudest jubilation—
As they prepare to die!

Soon, with wind's accompaniment,
They'll past my window fly—
Dressed for some bright destination,
They'll wave a glad "good-bye."

LORD, may my life, like autumn leaves,
Grow brighter, 'til the day,
When borne by Holy Spirit winds,
I too, shall fly away.

Grand Finale

Earth doesn't move to winter softly,
But with crescendo loud and lofty—
Her brilliant, firey tones entirely
Lavish—for the Grand Finale!

I wonder if the Church, like Autumn—
Her closing score's profuse display
Will dazzle earth with blazing glory,
Before her leaves are blown away!

"Arise, shine, for your light has come, and the glory of the Lord is risen upon you. For darkness shall cover the earth and gross darkness the people; but the Lord shall arise upon you and His glory shall be seen upon you."

(Isaiah 60:1-2)

Fall Stream

Late Winter Fog

Late winter snows meet warmer air—
Thick foggy mists enclose, and where
My mountains stood—there's nothing there!
(To sight, that is)
Because I know
My mountains have no place to go—
Until the day, that to and fro
The earth will reel, as mountains shake,
And crumble in the final quake.
So—though the mists my mountains make
Invisible—they stand in place.

Though mists obscure my Father's face—
Dark circumstance, His form erase,
My feelings shake—
Then Faith insists,
"He's standing there, within the mists."

"There is a River"

Apology

Dear, dear Earth,
You blow and break your branches off;
You heave and crack your crust;
You twist with turmoil from your bonds;
Hot lava fires you thrust
Past crevices we call your "faults"—
But NO! The "<u>fault</u>" is ours—
<u>We</u> sinned, Oh Earth,—In Adam's fall
<u>We</u> bruised your pristine powers!
<u>We</u> marred your uncorrupted soil;
<u>We</u> spoiled—and shared our fate
Of bondages, decay and death—

And yet—a glorious state
Of liberty awaits us—when
All shackled will be free—
And we, who caused your grief may speak
Long-due apology!

". . . this creation will be set free from the bondage of decay into the glorious freedom of the children of God.

… we know that all creation groans and travails together until now…"

(Romans 8:21-22)

SEA

Waters' Edge

*I walk the sand beside the sea—
My footsteps parallel the line
    Where two worlds meet—
Sea and Land—distinctive, wondrous worlds apart.
Sea creatures beach themselves on land—and die;
While we, the human kind, engage the sea,
But cannot long remain,
Ill-suited as we are.*

*The sun's reflection on the sea
Accompanies me as bright companion—
    Sparkling, changing into rippling patterns.
The light of both these worlds,
    So close by me.*

*LIGHT of earth and Heaven,
LORD JESUS, walk with me.
May my earth-bound trail beside Your "Other" world
Be close enough to "waters' edge"
To feel its breezes,
    See its patterns,
And know the brightness of the One
Whose shining warms my world
And draws and fits me ready
    For the next.*

Lupine on the Maine Coast

Preference

I think I'd like the Maine coast, Lord—
When judgment has subsided—
When plowshares will be formed from swords,
And earth—to saints, divided.

*While on a quick "get-away" to Cape Porpoise, Maine, I visited "Tillies" which was a typical grey, wooden "shack" beside a pier to which the lobstermen delivered their delicious treasures. I had just sat down on the rough picnic table on the pier with my steaming lobster, when—
I had an unexpected guest!*

Dinner Guest

Herring Gull—my dinner guest
At Tillie's shanty on the pier—
You eye my lobster with request—
Yet you're a native—I am here
As only tourist, passer-by.
You eat more lobster than do I!

We stare. Two worlds meet in our eyes.
I wonder where your path has led,
Free soaring through unbounded skies—
I drive macadam trails instead.

But our paths crossed, on Tillie's pier—
Free-flying gull, and earthbound I.
We share our dockside dinner here—
We voyagers—of earth, and sky.

At Rockport, Massachusetts, there is a delightful strudel shop, with a balcony overlooking the harbor. Here one may enjoy the delectable combination of coffee, strudel and a view of the water. As I was savoring my first bite of the melt-in-your-mouth sweetness, I had a visitor.

To: The Seagull at Rockport's Strudel Shop,
Fine Feathered Friend

Fine, feathered Friend, I'm glad we've met
Here on the balcony.

But I suspect you've come to get
More than my company!
In case you dare to grab my fare,
Intimidation futile—
Despite your beak and beady stare—
You may not have my strudel!

Winter Shore

Winter Shore, your blustery winds
Convey your beach to me.
We walk and talk on snow and sand
Sharing your resplendent strand
With only pebbles, washed and cleansed—
Sunbathing with their rocky friends.

Gone, the multitude of those
Vacationers who came,
Supposing they enjoyed the best
You offer—yet we know the rest
Of days devoid of chatting crowds,
Those private days when whipped cream clouds
And you and I and seagulls come
To watch your waters meet the sun.

To watch you in your sunrise dress
Of artists' colors, and to bless
Your after-glow, in sunset's light,
When weary sun gets tucked beneath
The ocean blankets, for the night.

Winter Shore, we share the best—
When chilly winds blow all away
But loyal friends who choose to stay;
Who love you—love your sparkling ways—
And walk with you on winter days.

Drops of Distinction

Little Wave within the sea,
Your problem of identity
Might be profound—
As well we know, who dwell
In oceans of humanity.

Yet—cosmopolitan your clan!
Pioneer drops since seas began
To wash the world-wide shores—
You house Ambassadors
From every Isle of Man!

So, Little Wave within the sea,
Splash tall—you hold
Nobility!

Sunrise with Sanderlings

We walk the beach at sunrise,
These sanderlings with me—
Expectant of a new surprise,
A gifting from the sea.

He gives them food—they scurry for
The latest treat he brings—
He gives to me a pelican,
And laughing gulls, on wings.

Then, on his waves, he sets a path
Of sparkling gold, to run
Right from my feet, across the sea,
Into the rising sun!

Someday, Lord, when time has come
To cross that trail to Thee—
I'll come with joy—but may I bring
These sanderlings with me?

Sunrise

Sunrise Surprise

*The Father holds behind His back
A gift, as a surprise—
It's wrapped with golden ribbons curling
Through pink and purple skies.*

*He lifts it to horizon's rim—
"Here my child, it's new—
A day long-planned, gift wrapped with love,
From My heart, for you."*

Resistance

Great boulders which comprise the ramparts of a shore
Seem stubbornly resistant to the sea—
Yet meet, continually, unaltered action's will—
Until—the rocks are pebbles; pebbles, sand—
And sand is washed away beneath the tide.

When stone defenses on the shoreline of my soul
Determine to resist Thy seas of grace—
Persist—in pulverizing unsubmissive will—
Until—my rocks are pebbles; pebbles, sand—
And all the sands of self are lost in Thee.

Storm at Sea

*"He hushes the storm to a calm,
so that the waves of the sea are stilled."*

(Psalm 107:29)

Simon Says—

"You want my boat?
Yes, Master, Come, I'll shove it from the shore so You may teach."

Then, to himself, complains,

> "He interrupts my necessary chores! They <u>must</u> be done!
> But… I'll comply. I feel I owe Him this for what He did—
> With my wife's mother healed, this favor's small.
>
> Just don't talk long! Your world is one of words—
> But mine is <u>work</u>—a smelly scene where
> Rotting entrails <u>reek</u> from fish I clean;
> Where nets demand my time.
>
> You speak of heaven—and so may I someday,
> But not just yet!
> For now my mind pursues elusive fish
> Throughout this sea—
> A nightly contest won by <u>them</u> last night!
> But You don't know discouragement like that!
> Nor how it feels when shoulders ache
> From straining oars against a vicious wind.
> I'm tired! But You don't understand."

> "At last He's through!"

"What's that? You say go out again for fish?"

> "I'll hold my tongue."

"Yes, Master, we will go."

> "He knows we've been at this all night!
> I told Him that!
> Then <u>why</u> this futile trip?
> I'll bow to His audacity to show respect…

But can't He see—-my rugged hands attest

My competence!
I know the ways of fish! To search for them by day—-
RIDICULOUS!
Yes, even such a man of God
Should stay within His field!"

What pounds my boat?
What churns these waters, slaps the hull
As some sea-monster's tail?

It's FISH!
We're riding <u>waves</u> of countless fish!

MASTER! FISH!"

Invitation

Come, says the Sea—
Come walk with me.
Release to me anxiety
And contemplate the vastness of
Eternity—beyond horizon's reach.

I tell of timelessness—
Of broad terrains
Of life and truth beyond earth's frame.

So rest, tired one—
Give me your feet—
Stretch out your weary heart
To the soothing washings of my waves.

Emerging

The Blue Sea

"Today"

*"Today if you will hear His voice,
harden not your heart."*

(Hebrews 3:15)

As drops assembled in a rushing wave
        Are soon dispersed, and never reconvene—

This group of rushing moments called "today"
        Breaks on the shore and never comes again.

SCRIPTURE

"Where shall I go from Your Spirit?

Oh where shall I flee from Your presence?

. . . If I take the wings of the morning

or dwell in the uttermost parts of the sea,

even there shall Your hand lead me

and Your right hand shall hold me."

(Psalm 139:7-10)

"Where shall I go from Your Spirit?

Breath of Beauty

Breath of Beauty,
Creating wondrous worlds and sparkling galaxies,
Breathe on me.

Breath of Ancient Origins,
Birthing light and lavish cosmic entities,
Breathe on me.

That sounds and shapes of artistry from Heart Eternal's repertoire,
May formulate, be seen, be heard
Throughout the earth.

That even wisps of Heaven's thought, through Alpha and Omega's voice
May be transformed to solid rock realities
Upon this earth.

That Love's divine expressions—from Father's heart
Through Word of Word incarnate,
By Holy Spirit's power—

May actualize into: "Your Kingdom come, Your will be done—
On earth, as it is
In Heaven."

For Your glory, Jesus—
Breathe on <u>us!</u>

"Alpha and Omega" I

Jesus said: ***"I am the Alpha, and the Omega,
The First and the Last!"***

(Revelation 1:11)

"Alpha and Omega" II

"He (Jesus) is the exact likeness of the unseen God. He is the firstborn of all creation.
For it is by Him that all things were created,
in heaven and on earth—things seen and unseen—
thrones, dominions, rulers and authorities—
All things exist through Him, and by Him and for Him.
He Himself existed before all things,
And in Him all things are held together."

(Colossians 1:15-17)

"I AM the Alpha and Omega"

*"Moses said to God, When I come to the Israelites and say that the God of your fathers has sent me, and they say,
What is His name? What shall I say?
And God said to Moses,
I AM WHO I AM...
This is My name forever."*

(Exodus 3:13-15)

*"He (Jesus) said to me I am the Alpha and the Omega,
The Beginning and the End.
To the thirsty I will give water from the fountain
of the water of life."*

(Revelation 21:6)

Close Call

"The Lord saw that the wickedness of man was great in the earth...
their thinking only evil continually,
and He regretted that He had made man, and was grieved at heart.
So the Lord said, I will destroy mankind from the face of the earth—
Not only man but beasts and creeping things and the birds of the air,
For I regret that I have made them.
But Noah found grace in the eyes of the Lord..." (Genesis 6:5-8)

Sad, brokenhearted, grieving God—
With all His efforts spent creating,
With all His loving thoughts relating
To Redemptions plan for man—

Now His heart is contemplating
Wiping out, even decimating
Earth, its putrid evils reigning—
Its wickedness, with no restraining.

Now—all mankind, all beasts and birds
To be destroyed—no longer heard
Will be their song, their last note played—
As earth, in perilous balance weighed.

God—with wounded heart regretting
That He <u>made</u> man—was He forgetting
The days designed for you and me?
Would we even, ever <u>be</u>?

"BUT NOAH..."

So—History hanging by a thread
Pivots on that simple phrase—
Earth holds its breath, her silence says,
"Is this my final, end of days?"

God looked at Noah, who walked with Him
As righteous friend—So grace was found.
And God rescinded; edict amended—
One faithful friend turned earth around.

Look Up!

Noah's Ark

**The door was shut by God—
Safety's guarantee—
The only window faced,
Not toward the surging sea
But Heavenward—its view—
Direction—Fear allays
Oriented to the Throne—
Not circumstance, nor waves.**

The Soldier

The soldier's job is grim—
But strength is not revealed in easy tasks.
His hammer is to drive the heavy nails
Into the hands and feet of men who soon
Will curse him savagely, as dearth prevails.
A scene familiar now.

His duty soon begins.
Now hard, from knowing death's companionship,
Ignoring hatred in the eyes of two—
The soldier startles at the voice he hears,
"Forgive them, for they know not what they do."
Forgiveness from condemned?

He stands transfixed and stunned.
No sword could penetrate as do the eyes
At which the soldier stares; his heart is bound
Far tighter than his victim's yielding hands.
The spike is placed.
The hammer's blows resound.
The task is now complete.

The crosses now are raised.
As enemies revile and while friends weep,
He watches silently, as Jesus dies.
One speaks, "This truly was the Son of God!"
The soldier's stoic countenance belies

The echo in his heart.

For Me

Ram in the Thicket

"Abraham raised his eyes and looked, and behold, a ram caught in the thicket by his horns; and Abraham took the ram and offered it up for a burnt offering in the place of his son.

(Genesis 22: 7-13)

Ram, in thorny thicket caught—

Prepared by God for sacrifice—

Sweet Isaac, to the altar bound,

Now finds release—

A substitute is found.

Jesus—Dying Lamb of God—

With thorns (the curse of sin) your head is crowned.

RAM—in thorny thicket caught—

<u>My</u> substitute is found.

Released and free, in gratitude I bow—

Your thorn-torn head

Is crowned with glory now!

The Lamb, Slain

In this painting, I wanted to express the correlation between the prophetic events of the Old Testament, and their fulfillment in the death of Christ. Beginning with the ram caught in the thicket, then the slain lamb and its blood on the doorpost of the Passover, and next in the ceremonial lamb on the brazen altar in the feast of Passover, we see the fulfillment in the cross of Christ and the blood moon.
From Christ's side flow blood and water—-the blood of the Lamb for our salvation and the waters of the Holy Spirit for our empowerment for living.

The chalice is an invitation for us to partake of the forgiveness and full salvation we are offered.

Broken Bread

BREAD of EARTH, produced by grains, hard-crushed—
And ground by stones, to where your floured form
No longer bears the shape of grain—Yet in your brokenness
You offer all mankind rich elements of sun and soil.

You give yourself to us, into our hands
Which pound and press, and knead your yielded form;
And to our fires—with hottest coals.
Yet through your sacrifice, we eat.

BREAD of HEAVEN, You too were crushed to where
Your anguished form was hammered, struck and marred.
Your sinless soul was pounded—ground by stones
With weight of all our sin.

Yet through Your brokenness, we share Your life.
You give Yourself, into our hands
Which stripped You—lashed You, "Hailed" You mockingly;
And to our fires of hate—those scalding flames
Which scorched and seared Your bleeding flesh.
Yet through Your sacrifice—we eat of Grace.

Your sacred Word is BREAD—
White hot with purging fire to light our path.
Your Word, from which cascading cleansing waters flow
With Holy Sprit's power, creating worlds and life.
Your Living Word is Jesus, Who places in our weak but willing hands,
The Living Bread, and says,
"Go, feed My sheep."

In this painting I have tried to express the twisted mockery of the Crown of Thorns. A royal crown and the colors of gold and jewels befitting a king— our King Jesus—here are broken and contorted in hateful ridicule.

Crown of Thorns

The Thorn

*The thorn first grew in curse of stony ground,
Surrounding Eden's once abundant lands*

*Where Adam basked in unbarbed beauty.
Now, sin's flower rips
His bruised and weary hands.*

*An unknown hand removes a twisted crown
From Jesus' brow in which its spikes had pressed.*

*Again—the curse of stony, blood-stained ground,
Thorns lie discarded
On Golgotha's crest.*

"He is Risen!"

"On the first day of the week, the women went to the tomb. . .and found the stone rolled back. When they went inside they did not find the body of the Lord Jesus. Two men in dazzling raiment suddenly stood beside them . . .and said to them, He is not here, for He has risen!"

(Luke 24:1-6)

"I Am the Resurrection and the Life"

"Jesus said. . .I am the Resurrection and the Life. Whoever believes on Me, even though he may die, he shall live."

(John 11:25)

The Stones Cry Out

This silent churchyard would not be so hushed
Were tombstones given songs—
For they would sing their temporary state—
And choirs of marble monuments would chant
"We wait the trumpet sound! For then, this ground
Will tremble with a power earth once knew—
(A hidden memory within our veins—
Another stone—our prototype—was moved;
Death's weight dislodged—The Resurrection, proved!"

"One day our polished faces will reflect
A holy light—as heavenly shapes ascend—
Amid the swirling mists, our empty tombs
And toppled forms will mark a place of LIFE!
(A hidden hope implanted in our veins)

For Christ will clear Death's atmosphere—
Destroy its gloom—
With winds of Resurrection joy!"

This silent churchyard would resound with praise,
Were tombstones given songs!

"Waiting for the Trumpet"

". . .a trumpet shall sound and the dead shall be raised. . ."

(I Corinthians 15:52)

The Stained Glass Window

Historically, the banner as a symbol of victory, alludes to the Emperor Constantine, who upon his conversion to Christianity, added the cross to his triumphant flag.

In Christian art, particularly in that of the Renaissance, the banner is used to symbolize Christ's victory over death. He is portrayed carrying the banner as He arises from the grave, in the descent into hell, and in His appearances after the Resurrection, prior to the ascension.

In the design for this stained glass window, the banner of the Resurrection is pictured surrounding and encompassing the cross, the symbol of death.
I wished to express in visual form the words of Scripture written in the open Bible below.

"When the perishable puts on the imperishable and the mortal puts on immortality, then shall come to pass the saying that is written:

Death is swallowed up in victory.
O Death, where is your victory? (Isaiah 25:8)
O Death, where is your sting? (Hosea 13:14)

The sting of death is sin, and the strength of sin is the Law.
But thanks be to God Who gives us the victory
Through our Lord Jesus Christ!"

(I Corinthians 15:54-56)

(I did only the design and cut the full-sized pattern for this 18' x 6' window which is in the sanctuary of the Three Village Church of East Setauket, New York. The actual construction of the window was done by Somers Studio on Long Island, New York. During that time I was allowed to critique the selection of the glass, to ensure that it matched the colors of my design. It was a rare privilege.)

"Death is Swallowed Up in Victory"

**The stained glass window in the
The Three Village Church, East Setauket, New York**

Two Gateways

Sealed and Shut

(Matthew 27:64-66; Ezekiel 43:1-7; 44:1-3)

Both sealed and shut with massive stones enclosing—
The Garden Tomb; Jerusalem's Golden Gate—
One closing IN Messiah's lifeless body;
One closing OUT prophetic words relating
To Messiah King, Whose triumphant entry
Shall shatter nations as His shout is heard—
As empires topple, evil armies crumble
Before the earthquake power of His mighty Word,

Rough Roman soldiers sealed the Garden Tomb;
Islamic Sultan Suleiman walled the Golden Gate,*
Believing their authority had conquered,
Their pompous power was controlling fate.

But holy laughter filled the courts of Heaven,
Forseeing what these soldiers' deeds portend—
The Garden Stone would roll, reveal Christ's ABSENCE,
The stones of Eastern Gate will fall, TO LET HIM IN!

"Lift up your heads, O you gates,
lift them up, you everlasting doors,
And the King of Glory may come in!
Who is this King of Glory? The Lord of Hosts—
He is the King of Glory!"

(Psalm 24:9-10)

*(1542-43)

"Sealed and Shut"

The River Flows

"Behold waters flowed out from under the threshold of the temple facing east. . . .It was a River. . . .Wherever the River goes, everything shall live." (Ezekiel 47:1-9)

Hosanna!

*Tribulations' fires extinguished—
Menorah's central candle, lit—
Fresh waters from the temple, gushing
Toward the Mount of Olives, split
By touch of feet which walked on waters;
By shout; by blast of trumpet's sound—
The River rushes to the valleys,
Bringing life to death-drenched ground.*

*Jerusalem's Eastern Gate re-opened—
Welcome, JESUS! Messiah, King!
Rule and Reign, Triumphant Savior—
Now, "O Death, where is your sting?"*

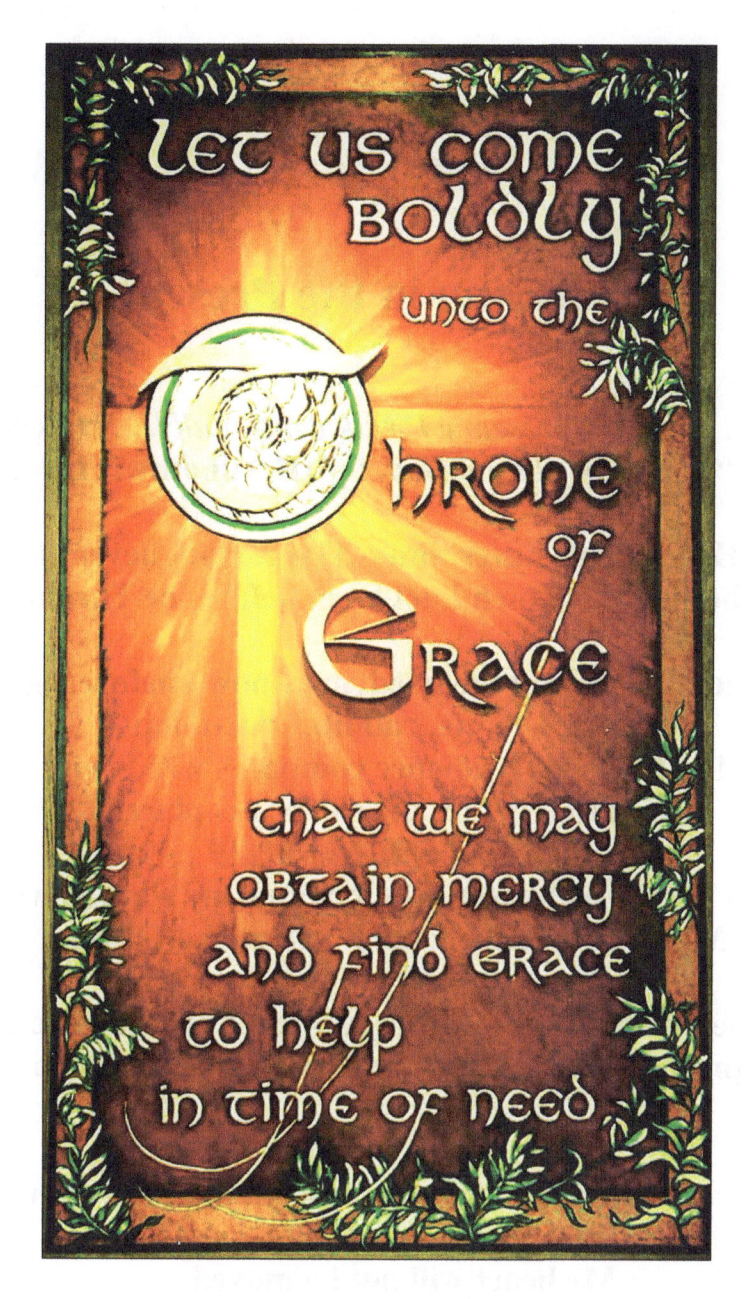

"Come to the Throne"
(Hebrews 4:16)

This altarpiece was painted for the prayer chapel of Gordon-Conwell Theological Seminary, South Hamilton, Massachusettss. Master artist Peter Granucci of Gilsum, New Hampshire, sculpted and water-gilded the gold leaf circle behind the "T" of "Throne."

Performing in the Presence

"The Lord... in Whose presence I walk continually..." (Genesis 24:40)
"...approved unto God..." (II Timothy 2:15)

The House lights never dim—The curtain never closes.
The stage on which I act is set before the Throne.

My lines, though unrehearsed, are known before I speak.
My role—to me, "ad lib," "ex-temp—
The Godhead Audience compares with script
Prepared before the earth was placed.

And They—with laser eyes, critique my soul, as well.
My motives, naked stand before the Throne.

But if, perchance, the Godhead Audience applaud the play—
If pre-planned script and my performance blend—

What more could any actor ask? What matter then
If earth's reviews congratulate, or castigate—
My heart will not be moved—

If my performance for the Throne,
The Godhead calls, "approved."

"Holy, Holy, Holy. . ."

Behold, a throne stood in heaven, with One seated on the throne. . . encircling the throne was a bow of emerald. . .from the throne came flashes of lightning. . .in front of the throne there was a glassy sea. . .

Around the throne were four living creatures—one like a lion. . .the second like an ox. . . the third had the face of a man, and the fourth, an eagle. . .They never stopped saying "Holy, Holy, Holy is the Lord God Almighty, Who was, and is, and is to come." **(Revelation 4:2-8)**

Sailing toward the City

". . .looking for the City whose Builder and Maker is God."

(Hebrews 11:10)

First Love

I want to gaze, not glance upon Your face—
Throughout my days, to dance
In Your embrace.

When midnight strikes, and Time on cue
Lowers his brisk baton,
Forever, in far grander hall,
To music of celestial ball,

The dance will still go on.

"Let my Beloved come quickly and take me to our waiting home upon the mountain of spices."

(Song of Solomon 8:14)

CPSIA information can be obtained at www.ICGtesting.com
Printed in the USA
LVOW02s1357020115

421233LV00004B/32/P